MEET
CHRISTOPHER COLUMBUS

MEET

CHRISTOPHER

COLUMBUS

★ ★ ★ ★

By James T. de Kay
Illustrated by John Edens

STEP-UP BOOKS

Random House 🏠 New York

To Sasha Cooke

First paperback edition, 1989

Text copyright © 1968 by Random House, Inc. Interior illustrations copyright © 1989 by John Edens. Cover illustration copyright © 1989 by Stephen Marchesi. All rights reserved under International and Pan-American Copyright Conventions. Published in the United States by Random House, Inc., New York, and simultaneously in Canada by Random House of Canada Limited, Toronto.

Library of Congress Cataloging-in-Publication Data:
De Kay, James T. Meet Christopher Columbus / written by James T. de Kay ; illustrated by John Edens. p. cm.—(Step-up biographies) SUMMARY: An easy-to-read biography of the sailor who never fully recognized the importance of his discovery which changed history. ISBN: 0-394-81963-2 (pbk.); 0-394-91963-7 (lib. bdg.)
1. Columbus, Christopher—Juvenile literature. 2. Explorers—America—Biography—Juvenile literature. 3. Explorers—Spain—Biography—Juvenile literature. 4. America—Discovery and exploration—Spanish—Juvenile literature. [1. Columbus, Christopher. 2. Explorers. 3. America—Discovery and exploration—Spanish.] I. Edens, John, ill. II. Title. III. Series. E111.D28 1989 970.01'5—dc19 88-19068

Manufactured in the United States of America 1 2 3 4 5 6 7 8 9 0

CONTENTS

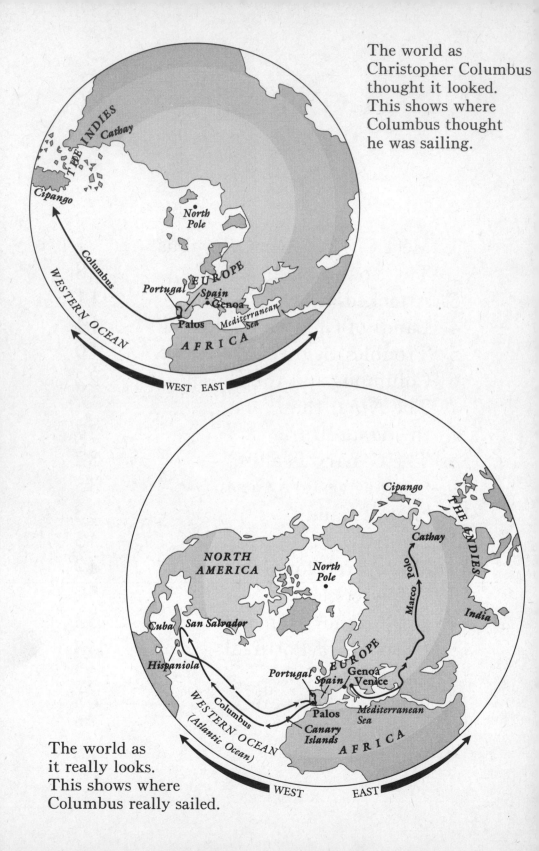

The world as Christopher Columbus thought it looked. This shows where Columbus thought he was sailing.

The world as it really looks. This shows where Columbus really sailed.

1
MEET CHRISTOPHER COLUMBUS

Five hundred years ago people in Europe knew little about the world. They knew it was round. But they did not know how big it was. They knew of lands to the east. But they did not know how far away they were. They knew there was an ocean to the west. But they did not know how far it stretched. They did not think anyone had ever crossed it. And they were afraid to try.

But Christopher Columbus was not afraid. His dream was to cross the Western Ocean. He became one of the greatest explorers in history.

2

THE YOUNG SAILOR

About 500 years ago in the city of Genoa, Italy, lived a red-haired boy. His name was Christopher Columbus. He worked for his father making cloth. But he did not want to be a cloth maker all his life. He wanted to see new lands and have adventures. He wanted to be a sailor.

Genoa was a good place to learn about sailing. It was a busy port on the Mediterranean Sea. Sailing ships from many lands came there. The streets were filled with sailors and traders.

Christopher soon learned to sail. First he sailed in little boats just for the fun of

it. Then he sailed on big ships. He learned
all the things a sailor has to know. He
learned to tell a forecastle from a poop
deck. He learned about masts and sails
and yards. He learned about cleats and
rigging and all kinds of seagoing things.

By the time Christopher was 25
years old, he had sailed all over the

Mediterranean Sea. He had been to France, Africa, and Greece. He had seen strange cities. He had had many adventures.

Christopher's wish had come true. He was a sailor.

In the spring of 1476 there was some exciting news. Five ships were getting ready to leave Genoa. They were going to sail to England. England is far away from Genoa. It is far away from the Mediterranean Sea. The ships would have to sail out into the great Western Ocean. Then they would sail north, past the lands of Spain, Portugal, and France.

Christopher got a job on one of the ships. And in the spring of 1476 he sailed out of the Mediterranean.

For the first time Christopher saw the great, green Western Ocean.

3

ATTACKED AT SEA

One day Columbus heard a shout from a sailor high on a mast. The sailor was pointing at some ships. They were warships! They were coming closer and closer.

The guns on the warships boomed. Cannon balls smashed into the side of Columbus's ship. They tore into the ropes and sails. They knocked down the masts.

Columbus's ship had guns too. The sailors shot back at the warships. There was noise and smoke everywhere. And Columbus heard the screams of sailors hit by the cannon balls.

The fight lasted all day. Many men

were killed. Columbus was hurt. But he kept on fighting.

Then a terrible thing happened. His ship began to sink.

Columbus jumped into the sea. He grabbed an oar floating in the water. He started to swim. He swam for hours. When he got too tired, he rested on the oar. Then he swam some more.

At last, late at night, he reached land. He pulled himself up on the beach and rested. Some men came down to help him. They told him he was in the country of Portugal.

4

LANDS OF
GOLD AND SPICES

Christopher Columbus decided to stay in Portugal. He went to live near the big, busy port of Lisbon. He married. He and his wife had a baby boy. They named him Diego.

From Lisbon he sailed to many places. He sailed to Africa, which is hot, and Thule, which is cold. He sailed to England and Ireland, Flanders and Germany. He talked to men who had been to other lands. These men sailed into Lisbon in ships filled with pepper and ginger and cinnamon and cloves.

These things were called spices. Spices

made food taste much better. People would pay almost anything to get them.

The sailors bought the spices from people called Arabs. But everyone knew the

Arabs did not grow the spices. They got them from faraway lands named Cathay and India and Cipango. These lands were called the Indies. The Indies lay far away to the east of the Mediterranean.

Many men did not want to buy the spices from the Arabs. They wanted to go straight to the Indies. The spices were much cheaper there.

The best way to get there was to cross the lands owned by the Arabs. But the Arabs would not let anyone cross their lands.

There was another way to get to the Indies. It was across deserts and over mountains. This way was too long and too dangerous.

Any man who found a new way to the Indies would become rich.

Columbus was sure he could find a way. He studied maps. He read books about the Indies. One book he read over and over

was called *The Adventures of Marco Polo.*

Long before Columbus was born, Marco Polo went to the Indies. He crossed the deserts and mountains. He saw many wonderful things. He had many adventures.

In Cathay, Marco Polo met the Grand Khan. The Khan was a great emperor. His clothes were made of gold. His noblemen's robes were covered with jewels and pearls.

Polo heard about Cipango, where a

palace had a gold roof. He sailed to Annam and Java. He saw forests of ebony. He saw the diamond fields of Golconda and the pearls of Maabar. And he saw fields of spices: pepper and nutmeg, galingale and cloves.

From reading Marco Polo's book, Columbus tried to figure out how to get to the Indies. Marco Polo got there by going around the world to the east. Columbus knew the world was round. So he knew he could get there by going around the world the other way—to the west.

But the great Western Ocean lay to the west. How big was it? Could a man sail across it to the Indies? No one knew.

Columbus thought he could do it.

He started to make plans to sail to the Indies. When he was ready, he went to see the king of Portugal.

5

TROUBLES BEGIN

Columbus asked the king to give him some ships. He said he could cross the Western Ocean in a few weeks. He would find the island of Cipango with its gold-roofed palace. He would bring back the riches of the Indies for Portugal.

The king liked Columbus's plan. He asked his advisers what they thought of it.

The king's advisers studied the plan. They said they did not like it. They said that Columbus was wrong. They said that the Western Ocean was bigger than Columbus thought. It would take too long to cross it. A ship could not hold enough food for such a long voyage.

The king listened to his advisers. He told Columbus he would not give him the ships.

But Columbus did not give up. He decided to go to Spain. He hoped to find someone there to help him.

Columbus's wife had died. He and his son, Diego, went to the town of Palos, in Spain.

Columbus wanted to go on to the city of Seville. He left Diego with some holy men called monks. They promised to take care of him.

In Seville, Columbus talked to a rich man named Don Luís de la Cerda. Don Luís liked the plan. He said that he would give Columbus the ships for the voyage.

Don Luís thought he should tell Queen Isabella of Spain about the plan. He wrote to her. She was very interested. She asked Columbus to come and tell her more about it. If she liked it, she would give him the ships herself. If she did not like it, she would not let him go at all.

So Columbus packed his things again. He left to see the queen in the city of Córdoba. And so begins the longest and most unhappy part of his great adventure.

6

COLUMBUS
AND THE QUEEN

On January 20, 1486, Columbus arrived in Córdoba. He found that the king and queen had left. He had to wait three long months before they came back.

Finally, in April, Columbus met King Ferdinand and Queen Isabella.

He told them about his plan. He said that he could sail across the Western Ocean to the Indies. Would they give him the ships he needed?

Isabella told him he had to wait while her advisers studied the plan.

Columbus waited. He waited for weeks. He waited for months. He waited for years! But he could never get an answer from the queen. She was always too busy.

Columbus was very angry. Why should he wait around for the queen of Spain? He went back to the king of Portugal. But the king turned him down once again. Heartbroken, Columbus returned to Spain.

Another year passed, and another and another. Columbus ran out of money. He was shabby and tired. His red hair turned white. He had waited six years for an answer from the queen. At last he decided to go ask the king of France for help.

Columbus went to Palos to pick up Diego. There he got a letter. It was from Isabella. She wanted to see him! Columbus got on a mule. He rode quickly off to see the queen.

This time Isabella had wonderful news. She said she would help him. After all these years, Columbus would get his ships!

Isabella asked him what prize he wanted if he found the Indies. He told her he wanted gold and silver and pearls. He wanted to be called "Admiral of the Ocean Sea." And he wanted to be the governor of all the lands he found.

Isabella's advisers told her that Columbus wanted much too much. The queen said she would have to think about it.

Weeks went by. At last she made up her mind. She told him she would not help him. Columbus was angry. Of course he wanted a lot! What was wrong with that? If he found the Indies, Spain would be rich. Why shouldn't he be rich too? He was the one who had to face the dangers of the long voyage.

Columbus climbed onto his mule and rode away.

Columbus rode for a few miles. Then he heard someone riding up behind him. It was a messenger from the queen. She had changed her mind again. She would give him the ships. She would give him everything he asked for.

At last Christopher Columbus's great adventure could begin.

7

THE *NINA*, THE *PINTA*, THE *SANTA MARIA*

Now things started to happen very quickly. Columbus hurried back to Palos to get ready for the voyage.

One of the first men he saw was a sailor named Martín Alonso Pinzón. Pinzón was a thin, hungry-looking man. He was a friend of Columbus.

Pinzón said he wanted to sail with Columbus. Columbus was glad to have him. He did not know that they would become enemies by the end of the voyage.

The queen told the town of Palos to give Columbus two ships. The ships were called caravels. They were fast and easy to sail.

Their names were the *Niña* and the *Pinta*.

Columbus rented one other ship. She was bigger than the caravels. But she was not as fast. She was named the *Santa María*.

Columbus liked the *Niña* best. But he decided to go on the *Santa María* because she was bigger. Pinzón was captain of the *Pinta*. His brother was captain of the *Niña*.

It took ten busy weeks to get the ships ready. New sails were made. The sailors loaded the ships with fresh water and tools and guns. They took along pigs and chickens to eat. They took fishhooks and boathooks and baskets and ropes. They took things to give to the people of the Indies. There were beads and bells and little red caps.

The men hammered and sawed and painted. Soon all was ready.

In the evening of August 2, 1492, all the men went to the church. Then they said good-bye to their fathers and mothers and wives and children. They climbed aboard the ships.

Very early the next morning they pulled up anchor. The wind filled the sails. With a cheer, the men set sail for the Western Ocean. The great adventure had begun.

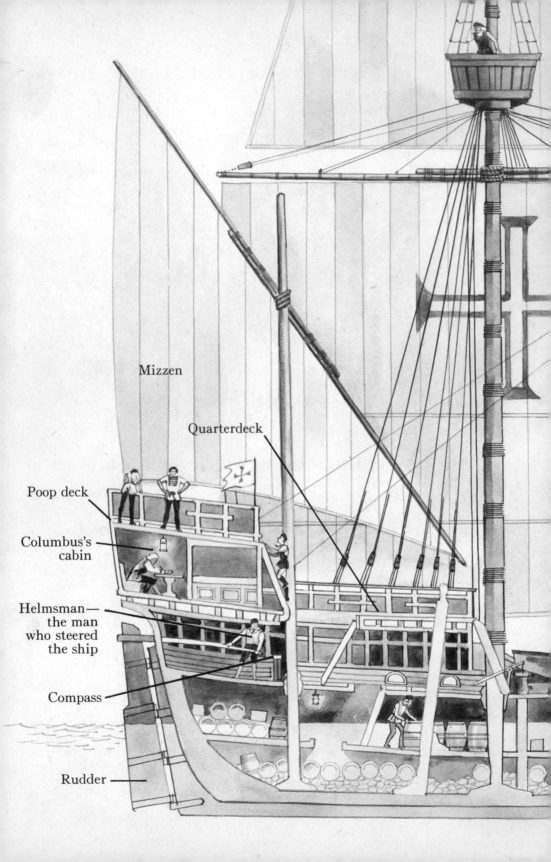

Mizzen

Quarterdeck

Poop deck

Columbus's
cabin

Helmsman—
the man
who steered
the ship

Compass

Rudder

THE SANTA MARIA

This was the ship in which Columbus set out to cross the Western Ocean. No one knows exactly what she looked like, but she was probably very much like the ship in this drawing.

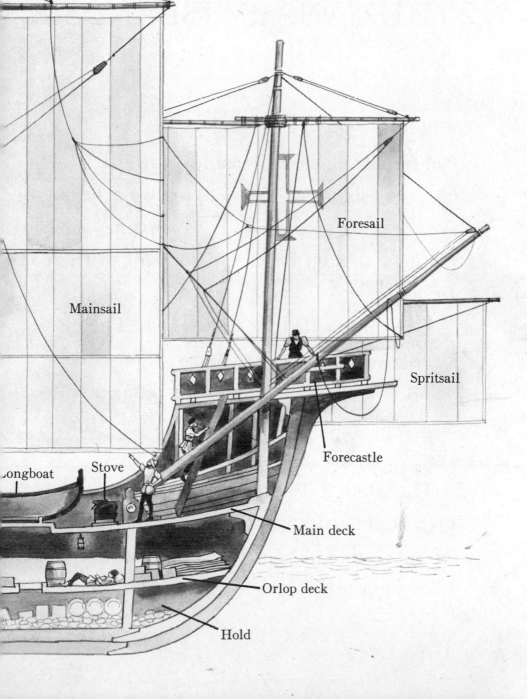

Foresail

Mainsail

Spritsail

Forecastle

Longboat   Stove

Main deck

Orlop deck

Hold

8

THE CANARY ISLANDS

Columbus headed the ships toward the Canary Islands. These islands were near Africa. They belonged to Spain. He planned to stop there on his way to the Indies.

The ships sailed for three days. Then a strong wind started to blow. The three small ships tossed and rolled. The waves smashed against them. Columbus saw that the *Pinta* was in trouble.

The *Pinta*'s rudder was broken. The men could not steer the ship. The *Santa María* could not help. The waves were too high for the two ships to come together.

32

Martín Alonso Pinzón fixed the rudder with ropes. But the ropes soon snapped. And the *Pinta* began to leak. Many of the sailors were afraid the ship would sink.

For another day they struggled through the heavy seas. Then early the next morning they saw land. It was one of the Canary Islands.

Pinzón and Columbus decided to separate for a few days. They did not think the *Pinta* could go on. They would look for another ship.

Columbus went to another island. But he could not find a new ship. He sailed back to meet Pinzón.

During the night the men saw a mountain that seemed to be on fire. They were very frightened. They said it was a sign that they would have bad luck. But Columbus had seen mountains like this before. He told them it was only a volcano.

Pinzón had not found a new ship either. So they set to work fixing up the *Pinta*. They fixed the leaks. They fixed the rudder. And they made better sails for the *Niña*.

When everything was ready, the three ships set sail once more into the Western Ocean.

9

ON THE WESTERN OCEAN

Columbus headed the three ships west. The sea was quiet. The sky was blue. Best of all, the wind blew briskly from behind them. It pushed the ships smoothly through the sea.

The men made fires on deck. They cooked hot suppers. This was a treat for them. In stormy weather they could not make fires. They had to eat their food cold.

Columbus was happy. His ships held enough food and water and wine to last his men for a year. He did not have to worry about their starving to death.

Columbus wrote down everything that happened during the voyage. He wrote about the weather. He wrote about the stars and the winds. He wrote about strange fish that swam around his ship.

He wrote about the birds that flew over-head. Often he worked far into the night. Sometimes he did not sleep at all.

Each day Columbus put down the number of miles they sailed. But he played a trick on the men. He wrote in two different books.

In one book Columbus wrote the real number of miles he thought they sailed. He did not show this book to the sailors.

In the other book Columbus wrote a shorter number of miles. He let the men see this book. He wanted them to think they were not too far from Spain. Then they would not worry so much.

Only Columbus knew how far, far away they really were from home.

10

"LAND! LAND!"

For about two weeks the ships sailed steadily on. The sky was clear. The air was fresh and clean. Then, slowly, the wind died.

The three small ships stood still in the middle of the ocean.

The men went swimming. The water felt wonderful. They had not had a bath for two weeks.

Soon the wind picked up again and the ships sailed on to the west.

The king had promised to give a prize to the first man to see land. Columbus was sure that land was near. Every man on each of the ships kept his eyes open.

One evening a shout came from the *Pinta.* Martín Alonso Pinzón called out that he saw land! The next morning everyone looked and looked. But there was no land to be seen. Pinzón had only seen a dark cloud that looked like land.

The sailors had not seen land for three weeks. They started to worry. Columbus brought out his book. It showed they were still near Spain. Even this did not cheer up the men.

They worried about the wind, too. It kept blowing them to the west. How could they ever sail east, back home to Spain?

Still they sailed on.

A few days later the *Niña* shot off a gun. This meant someone on the *Niña* had seen land. Everyone was very excited. But as the hours passed, the men saw nothing ahead but the sea.

The sailors worried even more. Would

they ever see land again? They became frightened and angry.

Every day they saw more and more birds. This made Columbus happy. He was sure these were land birds. It must mean that land was near. But the sailors did not care about birds. They just wanted to go home.

Columbus knew that the men were angry. He knew that they might try to kill him and sail home. But he had spent many years planning this voyage. Now he was sure he was near the Indies. And he was not going to give up.

One night the Pinzón brothers came over to the *Santa María*. They told Columbus they wanted to turn back too. Columbus said they would sail west for three more days. If they did not find land by then, he would decide about turning back.

For two days they saw nothing. But on the third night Columbus looked out into the darkness. Did he see a light?

Columbus was not sure. He told some of the sailors about it. They saw it too. But no one was sure it came from land.

Later that night the moon came up. Now the sailors could see the ocean clearly.

A sailor stood in the crow's nest high on the *Pinta*'s mast. He looked hard into the night.

"Land!" he shouted. "Land!"

The date was October 12, 1492.

11

SAN SALVADOR

And sure enough, land it was. The next morning Columbus sailed around it. He saw that it was an island. The hills and trees were beautiful. The air was filled with the smell of flowers. The sailors could see people on the island. The people wore no clothes. They came down to the beach to see the ships.

The sailors rowed Columbus to the shore. He stepped onto the beach. He got on his knees and said a prayer of thanks.

Columbus named the island San Salvador. He said it now belonged to Ferdinand and Isabella.

He tried to talk to the people on San Salvador. But they could not understand him.

Columbus could see that they were a friendly, happy people. They had no swords or knives or guns. Their skin was painted in bright colors. Some of them wore little gold rings in their noses. Columbus's eyes lit up when he saw the gold.

Columbus gave them tiny bells and little red caps. They gave him fresh water to drink and wonderful fruits to eat. They gave him some of their gold rings.

Columbus thought that the island was in the Indies. So he called the people Indians. But they were not like the Indians he had thought he would find. Where were their robes of jewels and pearls? Where were the palaces of gold?

He pointed to the gold rings they gave him. Where did the gold come from? Where was Cipango? Cathay? The Grand Khan?

The names Columbus used did not mean anything to the Indians. But they made signs to show him there were other islands nearby.

Columbus took six Indians back to the ships and set sail. ". . . I want to go and see if I can find the island of Cipango," he wrote in his book.

12

THE SEARCH FOR GOLD

Columbus sailed for weeks. He stopped at many islands. But there was no sign of Cipango or Cathay or the Grand Khan anywhere.

Finally he went to the big island called Cuba. The Indians in Cuba did a very funny thing. They rolled leaves into a tube. They called the tube a "tobacco." They put one end of the tobacco in their noses. They lit the other end and breathed in the smoke. Columbus thought this was very strange.

The Indians told Columbus there was a city on Cuba. A great king lived there.

Columbus thought this must be the Grand Khan at last. He sent two men to see him. They got all dressed up. They carried flags. And they took letters to the Khan from the king and queen of Spain.

Three days later they came back. They told Columbus there was no city. There were only a few houses. The roofs were made of leaves, not gold. And the chief they met was certainly not the Grand Khan.

The men said the Indians there thought the white men had come from heaven. The children had pinched them to see if they were real.

The Indians told Columbus about another island to the east. They called it Babeque. They said that its beaches were covered with gold. Columbus set sail for Babeque.

On the way there a strange thing hap-

pened. Columbus saw the *Pinta* sailing away from the other ships. He tried to catch up with her. But the *Santa María* was too slow.

Farther and farther away went the *Pinta*. Then Columbus knew what was happening. Pinzón wanted to be the first man to get to the golden beaches of Babeque. He was trying to beat Columbus there.

Columbus was furious. He knew he could never trust Pinzón again.

13

SHIPWRECK!

Strong winds blew the *Niña* and the *Santa María* away from Babeque. They came to the island of Hispaniola.

Columbus thought it was the most beautiful of all the islands.

The Indians were very friendly. They gave Columbus good bread and fresh water. They gave him bright red and yellow parrots. And they gave him pieces of gold. They had much more gold than the Indians on the other islands.

Columbus gave them lots of little bells and red caps and glass beads. He was very happy. He was sure that at long last, he had found the riches of the Indies.

The Indians told him about a place farther up the coast of Hispaniola called Cibao. They said he could find all the gold he wanted there. Columbus thought Cibao was the Indian name for Cipango. So on the day before Christmas, he set sail for Cibao.

At midnight that night, Columbus was sound asleep. Suddenly there was a terrible crunching noise. The *Santa María* had hit a huge rock! There was a big hole in the ship's bottom. Sea water was pouring in. Columbus and his men tried to save the ship. But it was too late. The *Santa María* was a wreck.

Columbus and his men rowed sadly over to the *Niña*. The *Santa María* would never sail again.

Columbus was worried. How were they all going to get home? There was not enough room on the *Niña*. He asked if any of the men wanted to stay on Hispaniola. Many said yes.

They built a fort. They made it out of pieces of the *Santa María*. Columbus called it La Navidad, the Spanish word for Christmas.

14

HEADING FOR HOME

Now Columbus decided he had to leave the Indies. He had only one ship left. If anything happened to the *Niña,* they would never get home.

Early in the morning of January 4, 1493, the *Niña* set sail from La Navidad. Columbus was heading for home at last.

For three days he sailed east, along the coast of Hispaniola. Then he saw a ship ahead. It was the *Pinta!*

Columbus sailed the *Niña* up to the *Pinta.* He was still angry with Pinzón. But he was glad to see the *Pinta.* It would be good to have two ships instead of just one for the long voyage home.

Pinzón told Columbus that there was no gold on Babeque. But he had brought lots of gold from Hispaniola.

Now the two ships sailed up the coast together. One day Columbus sent some men to shore for fresh water. They filled their barrels from a river. They saw something shiny in the barrels. It was gold dust!

Columbus said there must be a gold mine up the river. He named the river the River of Gold.

The ships sailed on to the east. In a few days they came to a small bay. Some of the men went ashore to find food. Suddenly more than 50 Indians jumped out from behind the trees. They had bows and arrows. They attacked the men. The men fought back. One Indian was hit by an arrow. Another was badly cut.

The Indians were surprised by the bravery of Columbus's men. They dropped their bows and ran away.

These were the only unfriendly Indians that Columbus's crew ever saw.

On January 16 the two ships left Hispaniola. They set sail for Spain across the Western Ocean.

For almost a month the trip went well. Then the wind grew stronger. It turned into a gale. The ships rolled and tossed in a great storm. Waves washed over the decks. Ropes and sails were torn away.

The next night the storm was even worse. The wind blew the *Pinta* far away from the *Niña*. By morning the *Pinta* was nowhere to be seen.

The storm did not let up. The men were terrified. They cried out to God for help. They promised that if they got to land they would go to church. They would wear only their shirts. And they would stay up all night giving thanks.

Columbus was afraid the *Niña* was going to sink. So he wrote down the story of his discoveries. He put the papers in a barrel. He threw the barrel into the sea. He hoped someone would find it. Then even if the ship went down, people would know he had found the Indies.

Another terrible day passed. Then the wind died down. And at last, far away, the men saw an island.

15
PRISONERS OF
PORTUGAL

It took three days to get to the island. There they dropped anchor.

There was a little church on the island. Columbus sent some men to pray there as they had promised.

The men rowed to land, wearing only their shirts. They went into the church. They knelt to pray.

Suddenly some men on horseback galloped up. They jumped down and ran into the church. They grabbed the sailors and dragged them off.

A little later a boat came out from land.

The captain of the island was in it. It stopped near the *Niña.*

The captain told Columbus that the sailors were prisoners. He said the island belonged to Portugal. The Spanish had no right to be there.

Columbus said that he was a very important man. He held up papers from the king and queen of Spain.

The captain yelled that he did not care about the king and queen. This island was Portuguese, he said, not Spanish. He told Columbus to sail to shore.

Columbus knew the captain would take him prisoner too. He yelled out that someday he would come back and punish him.

At last the captain gave in. If he could not get Columbus, he did not care about the other men. He let them go. When they were back on the *Niña,* Columbus sailed away.

But soon the worst storm of the whole

voyage hit the *Niña*. Huge waves battered the little ship. The wind seemed to lift her into the air. There was rain and thunder and lightning. The sails were ripped to pieces.

The storm lasted six long days. Then on the morning of March 4 Columbus saw land ahead. It was Portugal. He headed the *Niña* for a river. In she sailed, leaving the raging sea behind her.

16

AN ANGRY KING

People on shore watched the *Niña* fight her way in from the sea. Her sails were torn. She had been badly battered by the wind and the waves. But/she had made it through the terrible storm. She swept up the river, driven by the strong winds.

At last the *Niña* anchored near the city of Lisbon. People came to see her. She looked like a wreck. They could not believe she had sailed all the way across the Western Ocean.

Soon the king of Portugal sent for Columbus. Columbus did not want to go. Twice he had asked this king for ships.

And twice this king had turned him down. But Columbus did not dare say no to a king.

Columbus took some gold. He took some Indians he had brought back. He went to see the king.

He told the king he had found the Indies. He showed him the gold. He showed him the Indians. He said they were very clever people.

The king decided to give them a test. He called for a bowl of beans. He gave

the beans to one of the Indians. He asked the Indian to make a map of the Indies. The Indian used many beans to show all the islands. The king was amazed that there were so many islands. He was angry, too. He knew he could have owned them all if he had given Columbus the ships. Now they belonged to Spain!

The king hit his chest. He cried out, "Why did I let this great plan slip through my fingers?"

The king's advisers saw how angry he was. They told him that he should kill Columbus.

But the king said no. He was sure that Ferdinand and Isabella knew Columbus was in Portugal. They would know who had killed him.

A few days later, Columbus set sail again. The *Niña* sailed into the ocean, leaving Portugal behind.

17

THE HERO OF SPAIN

With all her flags flying, the *Niña* sailed up the river to Palos. The men fired off their guns. They were home at last.

It was Friday, March 15, 1493.

The people of Palos rushed to see the ship. They looked at the red and yellow parrots. They pinched and patted the Indians. And their eyes grew wide when they saw the gold.

That night another ship sailed up the river. She dropped anchor off Palos. Her captain stared unhappily at the *Niña*.

The ship was the *Pinta,* and her captain was Martín Alonso Pinzón. He had made it through the storm. He had reached the Spanish port of Bayona. From there he had sent a letter to Ferdinand and Isabella. It said that he had been to the Indies. He wanted to tell them about it.

But the king and queen did not want to see Pinzón. They wanted to wait for Columbus. They had told Pinzón not to come.

There had been nothing for him to do but sail home to Palos.

Pinzón was tired and sick. When he saw the *Niña,* he felt worse than ever. He knew Columbus would get all the gold and glory from the king and queen of Spain.

Pinzón could not face Columbus. He rowed to shore. He went home to bed. In a few days, Martín Alonso Pinzón was dead.

Columbus stayed in Palos for two

weeks. Then he went on to Seville. He had a wonderful time in Seville. People gave great parties for him. Everyone wanted to meet him. He was the hero of Spain.

18

ADMIRAL OF
THE OCEAN SEA

A week later Columbus set out for the city of Barcelona. He was going to see the king and queen.

Columbus took six Indians and some servants. He wore fine new clothes. The Indians were dressed in bright colors. They carried parrots in wooden cages. And they carried spices and fruits from the islands. The servants carried the gold.

It was a great parade. All along the way people came over to cheer the Admiral of the Ocean Sea.

At Barcelona, Columbus went to the beautiful royal palace. King Ferdinand

and Queen Isabella were waiting for him.

When he came in, Ferdinand and Isabella rose from their thrones to meet him. He knelt to kiss their hands. But they asked him to rise. They called for a chair and asked him to sit beside them.

The king and queen looked at the gold and the Indians. They listened in wonder to Columbus's stories of adventure. Then they all went to church to pray and sing. Tears of joy filled Columbus's eyes.

All his dreams had come true. He was rich. He was famous. And he had found a way to the Indies.

19
AMERICA

Columbus sailed west across the ocean three more times. He found many more islands. But he could never find the gold-roofed palace of Cipango or the pearls of Maabar.

At last he decided that the lands he had found were a part of the Indies that Marco Polo had never seen.

Soon other men were sailing west across the ocean. One of them was a man named Amerigo Vespucci. He decided that Columbus had not been to islands in the Indies after all. He said Columbus had found something even more important than a new way to the Indies. He had found new lands no one had ever heard of. He had found a whole "new world."

Vespucci was right. Soon people began to call this "new world" by a new name. They called it America, after Amerigo Vespucci.

Thousands of people crossed the ocean to America. This "new world" became new countries: the United States, Canada, Mexico, Brazil, and many others.

But all of this happened long after Christopher Columbus lived. For the rest of his life he believed he had found a new way to the Indies.

The last two years of Columbus's life were unhappy ones. Late in 1504 he came back from his last voyage. Three weeks later Queen Isabella died. King Ferdinand did not care about him anymore. Columbus had to fight for the prizes he had been promised for finding the Indies.

But the long voyages had tired him. He was sick and in great pain. He became weaker and weaker. And on May 20, 1506, he died.

Columbus had sailed thousands of miles. He had been to many strange lands. But his greatest adventure of all was his voyage with the *Niña,* the *Pinta,* and the *Santa María.*